Mr. Job

Ralph P. Karstedt

Ralph P. Karstedt

Fairway Press, Lima, Ohio

MR. JOB

FIRST EDITION
Copyright 1998 by
Ralph P. Karstedt

ISBN 0-7880-0968-0   PRINTED IN U .S.A.

Words, words, words!
Words about this, words about that,
Words about something, words about anything;
We speak, hear, write, and read words
And are seldom satisfied by them.

Words, words, words!
We use them to hurl questions into blackness
And strain to hear answering ones which never come;
Our lives are stuffed with discourse and chatter,
For even when all is spoken, our words go on and on.

Words, words, words!
Learned people employ them to tell us why -
Why nature's forces are violent and unruly,
Why cancers grow and pain refuses to depart,
And when their words are spent, the awfulness continues.

Words, words, words!
This little book is made of words.
They are words of questioning, words of searching,
Words forged by painful experience,
Words which wonder, words which ponder.

Words, words, words!
Is there no end of words?
Must we continually talk, ask, and never understand?
Is there no truth which rises from our verbiage?
Is there no word to satisfy our searching souls?

Words, words, words!
May God bless the words which lie within these pages
That they may be true to the life you and I share together
And be more than a shameless rattling of syllables,
May they somehow bring a collective word of hope and peace.

R.P.K.

"May the words of my mouth and the meditation of my heart be pleasing in Your sight, O Lord, my rock and my redeemer." (Psalms 19:14)

To Beth, with all my love.

TABLE OF CONTENTS

INTRODUCTION

So who hasn't heard about Job, his comforters, and his daughters? Job is the Biblical fellow who suffered a lot; his comforters asked dumb questions and gave bad advice; and his daughters were great lookers. Come to think of it, most of us think of "Job's Daughters" as a contemporary organization for young women of high school age.

We also know that "Job" is some sort of Bible book. We've heard about it. Maybe we've taken a crack at reading it. Only the toughest of us, though, have made it through all forty-two tedious chapters.

Relax! This little book is not a painful and exhaustive commentary on "Job." People far more learned and literate than I have written such volumes again, again, and again.

These pages are, rather, a commentary on life. They come from the struggle and pain Mr. Job and I have in common. They will meet you in the tough moments and impossible situations that you, I, and all creatures of this earth know far too well.

As writer and your guide, I promise no cheap trips or easy answers. As a matter of fact, we only fool ourselves and magnify our distress if we suppose such cheap and easy solutions exist.

We will take time for laughter along the way. After all, there is humor in everything, and those who don't take time to chuckle are likely to strangle on the juices of their experiences.

If you care to do so, you may pull your Bible from the shelf and search its pages for "Job." It's somewhere in the middle of the Old Testament. When you find it, you may want to glance through its several pages.

Take a look at the opening and closing sections. These are the parts of "Job" that everyone knows best. They are also the least significant paragraphs.

Take a hard look at the inner chapters. You'll probably get lost in a verbal fog, but you won't be the first to do so. I suspect Mr. Job, himself, was mightily confused by the circumlocution of his friends.

But this book is not really about "Job." It is about you, me, and our fellow strugglers in the affairs of this world. It is about cancer, heart disease, earthquakes, and tornadoes. It is about AIDS, the evening news, and the accidents our kids have at school.

This book is about life, and the search for understanding, and God. I'm getting interested in it myself. I think I'll read along with you.

J.B. AND ME

The bus pushed its nose through New Jersey fog. On its way west from New York City, it carried folks who had shared a night at the theater.

"J.B." is the play they had seen. Now as watches moved towards the witching-hour, sleepless riders discussed the thing they had viewed.

The play was a modern re-creation of an ancient Biblical story. J.B. was, in fact, Job transformed into the twentieth century. Those who had been mesmerized by the drama talked about the reality of it all.

"Do people really suffer like that?" The question moved from the front of the bus, to the back, and up to the front again. "Surely," many said, "the playwright exercised artistic imagination."

The pious spoke of Divine goodness. "We have to remember that the Lord is good. Things may seem tough for a while, but God's still on the throne." Their logic seemed irrefutable.

But others weren't convinced. "There is suffering in the world."

"How about Maude and her cancer?"

"Have you been reading the news out of Africa?"

The bus nosed on through heavy fog. One by one, passengers became drowsy. Only a few were left to carry on the after-curtain postmortem.

Then there was a lurch, a squeal of brakes, a spinning of the world of consciousness, a crash, silence, a moan, a cry. Those who survived that night were to remember "J.B." and know how graphically real its narrative was.

It all happened decades ago when "J.B." was a hot item on Broadway. For detailed information regarding the accident, consult the *New York Times*, or *The World*, or some other paper of the day.

J.B. is real. Those playgoers knew it. You and I are aware of it too. As a matter of fact, I have often thought of myself as a re-creation of the Old Testament character.

"Well, there lies our Job." The words were spoken by an adult Sunday School class-member. They were directed towards me.

The comment was somewhat understandable. I was just inside the classroom door, lying on a cot. Dressed in suit and tie, I had spent the previous hour conducting worship. Now, with aching back, I collapsed onto the cot in order to attend Sunday School.

But there is more, much more. In my head were a pair of plastic eyes. Hearing-aids rested in my ears. A bottle of nitro pills nested in my pocket. I looked a mess!

It had come upon me gradually. I was born in 1935 - a more or less normal kid. I couldn't see out of my right eye, but vision from the left side was reasonably adequate.

I got along fine during grade school years at Indianapolis' P.S. 72. My freshman year at Shortridge High School went okay, and then life began to dim.

The ophthalmologist said I had retinal hemorrhaging and separation. What I knew is that clouds of little dots and specks swam through my field of vision and curtained me away from the world I knew.

The process of going blind took nearly three years. I would have a bad spell, and then things would get better for a while. The clouds would come again, and they would be followed by a slight bit of clearing. Each cycle left me with less and less sight. When I went to bed at night, I never knew how much I would be able to see when I woke up in the morning.

I kept it all to myself. Not wanting to bother Mom and Dad, I simply struggled on. A couple of trips to the doctor were at my own expense.

I think a Michigan uncle knew a little about my struggle. He was bothered with a similar eye problem and regularly visited the Indianapolis doctor I consulted. I suspect Dr. Clark gave my uncle a ring, or at least, dropped him a note.

To the best of my knowledge, though, Mom and Dad didn't catch on to things until my sight was nearly gone. Maybe they had a notion of what was happening, and tried to hide the truth from themselves. I only know I traveled alone during three very tough years of high school.

The story of what came next is one I have often told. It involves high school graduation, college, a decision to enter the ministry, seminary, ordination, and marriage. Many of its paragraphs are laced with humor. Most of them tell of success.

While a seminary student, I learned the power of telling my story. In a speech class, I demonstrated a variety of items used by blind people and told a bit about my struggle with vision loss. Class members were fascinated, and my professor advised me to take the talk on the road.

That's how it all started. I spoke to service clubs, women's organizations, and at church services. I discovered that my blindness gave me a real opportunity to speak out concerning human capacities and the grace of God.

Then things began to happen again. On a fall morning in 1977 I awakened to discover a marked loss of hearing in my left ear. Scared half out of my wits, I made a speedy trip to our family doctor.

"Don't worry," Doc said to me. "I don't see anything wrong."

But the days of getting up to discover a lessening of hearing continued. They bothered me more than they might have disturbed the average person. After all, my ears were the instruments through which I "saw" the world. More importantly, each occurrence of loss reminded me of the awful days during which blindness had come upon me.

Years ago, in a college literature class, I was assigned a short-story, "The Death of Ivan Ilyitch." It was of Russian origin and spelled out the slow and inexorable way death had come upon a certain man named Ivan.

For some reason, Professor Cripe invited me to sit in front of the class and give my interpretation of the story. I began by telling of the long struggle I had experienced with the coming of blindness. I then likened my experiences to those of Ivan Ilyitch. The class was moved by my account, and I was too.

Well, it was happening again. At each real or imagined regression of hearing, skeletons rattled in my closet of memory.

There were times I seriously thought of taking my life. I wasn't ready to do it, but I foresaw a time when it might be thinkable.

I have long since come to terms with the lack of vision, but being both blind and deaf was, and is, my idea of earthly hell. I know, though, that suicide can never be an acceptable alternative for me.

Two decades have passed, and reasonably decent hearing has stayed with me. I am, however, still very conscious of my loss and am profoundly bothered by it.

Two other things happened. In 1987 I had a heart attack. Mary Evelyn and I spent our silver wedding anniversary with me bedfast in an Indianapolis hospital. I came home to cardio-rehab, a rather severe diet, and a serious program of exercise. It was a scary time, but I emerged from it pretty well.

Then a year later, there was an extended, and then ruptured, disk in my back. I had never experienced such pain. Those were the days when I was cot-bound and labeled Job.

But I've been reciting only the grim headlines of life. As a matter of fact, there have been plenty of bright times too.

We gained a daughter, Beth, in 1966; I have had a series of satisfying ministries; and all sorts of other good things happened as well.

For one thing, Mary Evelyn and I took up biking. One afternoon we were listening to a recorded book and heard the account of a blind fellow and his wife who rode together on a tandem. The idea struck fire with us, and we were off and riding.

A few years later, we took on leadership for a church oriented bike-camp for jr. highs. My wife gradually dropped away from the riding, but I stuck with it. With a number of front-end companions, I conducted nineteen of the annual camps.

Words can't describe the joy evoked by these biking weeks. We rode about 250 miles in five days and visited all sorts of interesting places. Each camp was an adventure for kids and counselors who went down the roads together.

Here's a bike-camp tale from a few years back. On Tuesday morning, Todd took a nasty spill and sprained his right wrist. We thought it was sprained, but it could have been fractured. The doctor who examined it put the wrist in a light cast and told Todd to have it checked in about a week.

Well, Tuesday evening of our biking camp was the time we have kids write letters home. With wrist in cast, Todd couldn't write by himself. He got an adult counselor to be his scribe and get the note on paper.

When Todd's mother picked him up Friday afternoon, she was convulsed with laughter. "I got this letter from Todd," she explained. "He said, 'We visited a beautiful church; we had an accident; Ralph is blind!'"

"Well," the mother continued, "when I read the letter, my first thought was: 'My God, what kind of accident did they have!' Now I understand."

There have been good days — lots of good days. Mary Evelyn and I have traveled broadly, and our shared life has been extremely rich. For the most part, being blind hasn't held me back a bit.

In the late '70s, I enrolled in a Doctor of Ministry program with Drew University of Madison, New Jersey. The enterprise called for a year of classroom study and the writing of a professional project paper. The paper, which in many programs is called a dissertation, was to have theological value and be rooted in some aspect of personal ministry.

The first subject I thought of was preaching. For years I have harbored a secret ambition of teaching young ministers how to preach. I majored in homiletics in seminary and am fascinated with the art of communicating faith from the person behind the pulpit to the people in the pews.

But what could I write about preaching that hadn't been said already? Preaching has been on this earth ever since Adam bawled out Eve for making indecent proposals with the forbidden fruit. Libraries are crammed with volumes written on the subject. What new insights could I hope to offer?

As I reviewed options, I thought again of my blindness. People were caught up in talks I gave on the subject. Although I certainly wasn't the only sightless pastor in creation, the number of us was relatively small.

I finally decided to examine the impact of my blindness upon my ministry at the church I was then serving. As a prelude to the study, I developed a theological interpretation of the effects handicapping conditions should have upon ministry.

The more I studied and the more I wrote, the more I became convinced that my lack of sight actually gave me a considerable number of advantages. It opened doors and allowed opportunities that might be denied a normal pastor. For me, the insight was stunning.

My study was, in fact, blazing a path through new territory. Zillions of books had been written about the things society should do in order to minister to the disabled. There was scarcely a volume, though, about the opportunities disabled individuals have to minister to general society.

How can blindness ever be thought of as an asset? For a detailed answer to the question you'll have to read my book, *As I See It.*

The volume you now hold in your hands, however, is a pretty good case in point. The fact that I have known the pain of struggle qualifies me to write it.

If the cook won't eat his food, you'd better approach the table with caution. If a writer about grief doesn't know what loss is, you have a right to ask questions. My blindness, and other ailments, qualify me as a sort of authority whose thoughts may be worth reading.

Here's another tale. It goes back to the Spring of 1980 when my United Methodist Church was preparing for its General Conference in Indianapolis. I was invited to be part of a task force assigned to make the conference site ready for disabled people.

I still remember the snowy, March morning we met at the Roberts Park Church in downtown Indy. We sat in the parlor and talked about everything: wheelchair cuts in Indianapolis curbs, the width of restroom doors, the availability of signing for the deaf, and floor-level seating for those who would find step climbing either difficult or impossible. By the time we left that meeting, we were convinced our General Conference would be ready and waiting for all its disabled visitors.

Then the first day of General Conference dawned. At the opening session Dr. Howard Rice of the United Presbyterian Church, U.S.A. came to offer fraternal greetings. The Presbyterians were saying "Howdy" to the Methodists.

Dr. Rice approached the speakers' platform in his wheelchair. Just guess who hadn't thought to put an access ramp up to the rostrum!

I could pour one account on top of another. Our society wants to be kind to its disabled members, but it really doesn't take them seriously as community leaders and contributors. I personally knew better, and I fell into the trap.

That's what my study was all about. I wanted to pave a way of understanding so that men, women, boys, and girls with physical limitations could have the opportunity to be significant leaders in their communities and congregations.

The idea is as old as Scripture's "Suffering Servant." Christ brought salvation through the pain of the cross. God often uses human suffering as the agency through which saving grace is transmitted.

By the Spring of 1981, my study was over and project paper written. My work was accepted, and I was awarded the diploma declaring me to be a Doctor Of Ministry.

There was a real ego trip. On that May morning, Mary Evelyn took a picture of me wearing doctoral garb. Someone else made a photo of her taking the picture. The second shot later appeared in a university publication.

One more step had to be taken. My project paper, "The Impact Of My Physical Blindness Upon My Ministry At The Burlington United Methodist Church," had a title long enough to gag a goat. Its hundred and ten pages of text weren't much more palatable.

A doctoral paper is written to sound learned and impress professors. It is composed with complex sentences and words of no fewer than four syllables. The harder it is to digest, the more scholarly it sounds.

I am, of course, exaggerating a little. The fact remains that my paper wasn't fit for general distribution. It was dry as a desert.

I began writing once more. I took the ideas of my paper and popularized them in a readable and relatively light form. The result was a small book, *As I See It*, which was published in 1985.

The book had a printing of two thousand copies and sold out quickly. Although I wish it had a far wider distribution, I know it has done much good.

A subtle change had come into my life. My handicap had ceased to be a handicap. I had found purpose for it and learned to use it as an implement of work and ministry.

Now I wonder. Does God keep jolting me with problems so I will remember who I am? The Lord never intended for Job to profit from his suffering. Is it possible God is giving me extra jabs and jars to keep me in my place?

I can't believe God would do something like that. On the

other hand, Mr. Job didn't think the Lord was capable of making things tough for him.

I should be ashamed for likening myself to my dear friend, Mr. Job. Job was, after all, denied virtually everything except the breath of life. I, on the other hand, live a pretty plush existence.

I draw a decent salary, ride in a comfortable car, am troubled by too much, rather than too little, food, and am a pretty contented fellow. I have long since come to terms with blindness and really don't object to a pair of hearing aids. The exercise program and low cholesterol diet are okay too. But my back has begun to trouble me again and the pain in my leg is fierce.

I climb sixteen steps as I ascend to our bedroom. On certain evenings, I drag myself up every one of them muttering, "Why does a person have to have pain like this?"

Well, I've told you a great deal about Ralph. I have done it in the belief that, somewhere along the line, you will have boarded my buggy.

Every one of us has hurts, heart-aches, pains, and problems which seem too much to bear. Every one of us has cried out, "Lord, what did I do to deserve all this?"

My acquaintance with J.B. is not just mine. With a multitude of variations, we have all been participants in the dramatic story.

So why do people struggle and suffer? Why is there pain in the world? Why is this globe visited with cancer, AIDS, wars, and tornadoes?

Along with Job, we hurl questions into eternal blackness. Sometimes we even listen for an answer.

Here's one more story. Back in 1984 our daughter, Beth, was getting ready for a trip to Sweden. She was to be an exchange student and would be gone for a year.

You can bet Pop wanted to talk with his daughter. We ended up taking a series of long, late-evening walks.

That particular June was miserably hot in Indiana. We couldn't work up energy to walk until after 10:00 P.M. Then we walked, talked, walked, and talked.

One Wednesday morning I had coffee with Pastor Jim, minister of the local Baptist church. Jim commented he had seen Beth and me walking past his church the previous evening.

"Oh yes," I responded. "We walk almost every night now."

I could hear a light switching on in Jim's brain. "Were you walking Monday evening?"

"Yes," I replied, "it's like I told you. We go out virtually every evening."

"Monday night," Jim questioned, "were the two of you out near the cemetery?"

I thought a moment. "Yes," I said, "we weren't out there very long, but we were there. We went in the east gate and came out the north."

"That explains it, "Jim chortled. "I was just talking to the town marshal. On Monday night he had a strange phone call. A lady said she had seen a bald-headed old man pushing a young girl into the cemetery. She said he and his cops had better get out there in a hurry. They went and didn't find a thing."

Well, if you'll let a bald-headed, old, blind-man be your guide, I'd like to lead the way into the darkness brought on by many questions and little understanding. Just turn the page, and here we go.

DON'T TELL ME WHY

"Hey, Joe," Arlene called. "Do you know why the blind guy gave up bungee jumping?" Her answer came quickly upon the question's heels. "Because it scared the heck out of his guide-dog!"

Both blind and wheelchair bound, Arlene sat among friends who circled a camp fire. She smiled at the laughter evoked by her joke. Then she began to strum her guitar and sing.

"Tell me why the stars do shine;
Tell me why the ivy twines;
Tell me why the sky's so blue;
And I will tell you just why I love you."

27

"Why" is the query of a child and the operative word of the human family. It is a sign of our curiosity and a driving force behind our accomplishments.

Children want to know why things are as they are. From humanity's youngest days, men and women have searched for knowledge that can enable them to live successfully in this world.

Why do the stars shine? Why does the sun rise in the east and set in the west. Why are some children born healthy and others with significant defects? Why? Why? Why?

The first sermon I ever preached was delivered under strained circumstances. Rev. Herman Emmert, our pastor, was out of town, and I — a young theology student — agreed to bring the Sunday message.

"Why" is the title I chose for my sermon. I proposed to deal with the whole issue of human suffering.

As things happened, I came down with a fierce head-cold on Saturday, the day before I was to preach. By the time I stepped into the pulpit, I had virtually lost my voice.

There I stood, a young blind man who could speak only in a hoarse whisper. And I dealt with the question, "Why?"

For more than one reason, folks in the pews leaned forward to catch every word. The message was probably sophomoric, but it was certainly heard attentively.

You and I want to know why bad things come our way — why there are tornadoes, earthquakes, cancers, and headaches.

The pains and inequities of life bother us, especially when they become personal.

Towards the close of the previous chapter, I mentioned that we sometimes really want to know why things happen. In writing those words, I was neither cynical nor trying to be a wise-guy. What I intended to imply is that the search for knowledge may not always be what our questioning is about.

"Why? Why, God, why? Just tell me why he had to die!"

Ruth blurted out the words as she was being led from the church. My heart ached for her, because I appreciated her pain.

Ruth's father, Frank, had died of a sudden and unexpected heart-attack. At the close of the funeral, the young woman shook with grief and hurled questions into the heavens.

Suddenly I realized no answer in heaven or earth would give Ruth satisfaction. Had the voice of God rumbled from on high, had the Lord explained Frank's death with painstaking, eternal logic, Ruth would not have been satisfied.

Her voice reminded me of a child's: "Mommy, why must I wear my sweater? Why do I have to drink my milk? Why must I go to Sunday School?"

No answer Mom can give will be sufficient. If she says her child will get sick if the sweater isn't worn, the reply will immediately come: "I won't either!"

Logic never satisfies a child who is displeased with conditions. "You're not right," is the rejoinder to all explanations.

In effect Ruth was subconsciously taking on the Lord in argument. Her words were an invitation to debate. Unable to accept her dad's passing, she was set on proving the Lord one hundred percent wrong.

I think of my grumbling trips up our stairs. "O God, why does anyone have to hurt like this?" The words are rhetorical. I don't expect an answer. I am hurting, and I am compelled to complain about the pain.

I remember Henry and Alice. They were members of my first church, and my very first funeral was for their three-year-old son.

Little Billy had been in the barnyard while his grandpa worked with the tractor. As the man climbed onto the machine and put it in reverse, the small boy ran out to get on board with his grandfather. A huge wheel ran right over Billy's head.

I got to the family home as quickly as I could. When Henry met me at the door, he embraced me and said, "Why, Ralph, why?"

At that moment he really didn't want an answer. His spirit and voice were complaining about eternal injustice. Things weren't right, and he didn't like it. Who could have blamed him?

I suspect a great percentage of questions regarding pain and grief are not really questions. They come from people who are grossly dissatisfied with events of their lives and who want to take on God in subconsciously motivated argument.

When we are removed from the immediacy of pain, though, we still ask the problem question. Why, indeed, is life crammed with inequity, grief, and untimely death?

Three types of answers are usually given to this sort of inquiry. Each of them holds truth. Each falls short of adequacy.

1. WE SUFFER FOR OUR SINS. This interpretation rises from experience and is shared among many people. It lies at the heart of the questioning cliche, "What did I do to deserve all this?"

The concept has obvious applications. A person gets drunk and wrecks his auto while trying to drive home. An employee is caught dipping from the company till and suddenly finds himself on the streets looking for work. A young athlete ignores his coach's curfew and is benched for the most important game of his life. A sexually irresponsible individual discovers he has AIDS.

Scripture is loaded with teachings that we suffer for our sins and are rewarded for virtues. "Honor your father and mother," one of the Ten Commandments tells us, "so that you may live long in the land that the Lord, your God, is giving you." (Exodus 20:12)

The teaching is paralleled in many passages. Do it right, and you will be blessed. Mess up, and punishment will come your way.

Our sins and mistakes do have consequences. We know it, and yet we don't. Deed and consequence are, in fact, often so far apart they are hard to recognize as belonging to each other.

"Brush your teeth, or you'll get cavities." Johnny doesn't see any truth in his mother's words. He didn't brush his teeth yesterday, and he doesn't have cavities this morning.

"Smoking may be injurious to your health." The Surgeon General may say it, but young people puff away knowing they are healthy and don't have cancer — at least not yet.

Delayed consequences often mask reality. It is like the proverbial fellow who challenges the law of gravity, steps from a high cliff, and is heard to say while falling, "So far, so good."

There is a relationship between the things we do and those which happen to us. Inappropriate actions and pain are definitely linked together.

But this style of thinking has some obvious, nasty twists. Sometimes folks suffer for the sins of others. Sometimes we compound their hurt by heaping guilt upon pain.

If a parent beats, sexually molests, or in some other way abuses his children, he may, in fact, end up in jail. The other side of the matter is that his sons and daughters are terribly damaged. Pop may deserve his punishment or even worse. The kids, though, haven't done a thing to warrant the shame, guilt, and pain which are inevitably theirs.

If a woman is attacked on the streets, society does its best to prove her responsible for the happening. "What was she doing out at that hour of the night?" "What business did she have in that part of town?" "She should have known better than to dress like that."

Somehow life seems more just if a person can be held responsible for the bad things which come to her. As a matter of fact, though, life doesn't always work that way.

Jennifer was driving home from school. She and two friends talked and laughed as the car rolled through autumn countryside.

Suddenly a truck, driven by a youth loaded with too many beers, streaked from a farm lane and struck Jennifer's auto in the side. The car rolled; doors were thrown open; bodies flew; and there was death.

"She should have been wearing a seat-belt," some folks said. Undoubtedly so, but the accident happened decades ago when few vehicles had safety restraints. The simple fact is that Jennifer was killed because of another person's drunkenness. She wasn't responsible for what happened.

I write these words shortly after a tragic air-crash in northwest Indiana. The day after the disaster, a local newscaster interviewed people preparing to board a plane and flight similar to the one which went down.

"I'm not afraid to fly," a woman said. "I'm a good Christian, and I know the Lord will take care of me."

I wondered about the sixty-eight men, women, boys, and girls who had just been killed in a rain-swept, Hoosier cornfield. Many of them, I speculated, were good Christians.

In 1965 a series of killer tornadoes swept through Indiana. One of them struck in the parish I was serving.

At one country crossroad, nine people were killed. Three homes were demolished, and an auto carrying a pair of honeymooners was picked up and hurled several hundred yards.

A dear member of our church lived only a quarter-mile north of the tragic corner. She later testified the Lord had saved her because of her faith.

"What about Earl's faith?" I wanted to scream. "What about those two young people who were in the first beautiful moments of marriage?"

Some theologians and philosophers say we are making the matter far too personal. They teach that humankind is punished for its collective sinfulness. Men and women of continuing generations have woven a life-fabric in which violence, deceit, injustice, and badgering egotism are basic components.

People, then, suffer because of society's sinful quality. Along the way, individuals are caught between grindstones of circumstance.

This societal interpretation of pain and evil is something we must talk about later. At the moment we are turned off by it. The approach seems to license evil and not be responsible to the question, "Why do John, Matilda, and Ralph experience the bad things which come as their lot in life?"

People are visited with troubles because of their blunders and sins. God has structured life with this inbuilt attempt at justice.

Yet all suffering can not be explained in such a manner. The teaching falls far short of unqualified truth. There has to be more, much more.

2. SUFFERING IS GOOD FOR US. I grit teeth while writing these words. Deep inside myself, though, I recognize their truth.

"No pain, no gain" is one way to tell the story. I smile at the thought. Each spring, when my friend, LeRoy, and I go out for our first biking expedition of the year, we learn all about pain.

A person who's going to do distance biking has to get used to a hard, narrow seat. Any experienced cyclist knows it is far the best seat for long-range touring. We also know a rider must ride, hurt, ride, and hurt some more until he, at last, has permanent calluses on his behind. That's the only way it works.

By the time June comes LeRoy and I are ready for fifty miles at a shot. Had we attempted such a trip back in March, we would have been candidates for hospitalization. Pain is part of growth. My biking soul knows it.

In younger years, I studied the violin. As a matter of fact, I once had aspirations of being a concert violinist. I pictured myself playing Bach and Beethoven on concert stages of the world.

Guess what! I had to practice, practice, and practice. I had to do it till my arm was tired and fingers sore. Talent is always necessary, but the discipline of practice is the basic component of a musician's accomplishments.

While in college and seminary, I was an honor student. I hadn't done so well in public school days, but they came before I lost my sight.

I started college scared. A fraternity which invited me to its rush-party really turned on my fear-juices. When the guys found out I was blind, they said they couldn't possibly have me on their house's roles. They were sure I was going to flunk out, and their fraternity's grade average was already too low.

So I was scared, and I worked. As a matter of fact, I worked so hard I went all the way to the top of the class.

These words are not written boastfully. Experience tells us disabled men and women are often honor-students in universities across the nation.

Lack of sight, hearing, dexterity, or mobility has somehow energized physically limited people to dig in their heels and go for the gold. Their weakness has, in fact, become the incentive which has propelled them towards success.

We've all seen it happen. The tough happenings of life have become the stuff and substance of growth.

Jesus often described life as being other than it seems. "Blessed are the poor in spirit, for theirs is the kingdom of heaven. Blessed are they that mourn, for they shall be comforted." (Matthew 5:3,4)

Christ had a profound understanding of life as we all live it. Poverty and pain can, in fact, be the substance of human growth. Deep inside ourselves we know it.

But it runs against our grain. We don't like to suffer, struggle, or experience pain. Such disagreeable things are at the bottom of our want-list.

Just look at the lines of people who are retiring at younger and younger ages. "If a person can draw a pension, why on earth should he work?"

In my more heady moments, I have actually thanked God for sending problems my way. I know they have made me the pastor and person I am.

But I don't really like it. I don't want to be Mr. Job. I wouldn't complain if the blessings of adversity were spread around with more equity!

3. GOD KNOWS BEST. This pious statement represents the third traditional explanation of grief.

I employed the concept of Divine knowledge at my first funeral. Do you remember Billy, who was killed in his family barnyard? I spoke of God's vast knowledge as I attempted to bring solace to Billy's grieving parents.

"For now we see in a mirror dimly, but then face to face." I quoted the well-loved text from 1 Corinthians 13.

"We can never understand eternal plans and purposes," I said at the funeral. "God's wisdom and mercy are far beyond our own. Someday, though, we will understand and even appreciate the Almighty's greater knowledge."

Looking back on that trying afternoon, I shudder just a little. I think of folks who say, "God needed another angel in heaven." The thought turns me off in a big way. What kind of God would deprive me, or Henry and Alice, or anyone of their child?

Towards the end of a forty-two chapter struggle to understand his suffering, Job finally complained bitterly to the Lord. God responded with an earthquake, whirlwind, and thundering of words. He confronted Job with the tough questions.

"'Who is this that darkens counsel by words without knowledge? Gird up your loins like a man, I will question you, and you shall declare to me.'"

"'Where were you when I laid the foundation of the earth? Tell me, if you have understanding. Who determined its measurements — surely you know! Or who stretched the line upon it? On what were its bases sunk, or who laid its cornerstone, when the morning stars sang together, and all the sons of God shouted for joy?'"

"'Or who shut in the sea with doors, when it burst forth from the womb; when I made clouds its garment, and thick darkness its swaddling band, and prescribed bounds for it, and set bars and doors, and said, "Thus far shall you come, and no farther, and here shall your proud waves be stayed?"'"

"'Have you commanded the morning since your days began, and caused the dawn to know its place, that it might take hold of the skirts of the earth, and the wicked be shaken out of it?'" (Job 38:1-13)

Having been thus addressed by God, Job fell on his spiritual knees. Who can blame him?

The Old Testament book begins with Mr. Job being tested with adversity. God wants to prove to Satan that his servant is truly good and faithful.

At the book's end, Mr. Job is returned to health, wealth, and good fortune. He is blessed with land, money, sons, and beautiful daughters.

Many Bible scholars teach that the opening and closing portions of Job are literary extensions which were added long after the text's central portion was written. They suspect the prologue and epilogue were composed to give an easy answer to the book's perplexing central question.

If scholars are right, the latter-day authors must have been dissatisfied with the answer, "God knows best." They tried to provide rational parameters for the text.

Since this is not a book of Biblical scholarship, I will say nothing more about the prologue and epilogue. Suffice it to say that, if God knows best, His knowledge remains a mystery to us mortals. Being the curious and profoundly concerned creatures we are, we continue to probe for truth.

"Tell me why the stars do shine." "Just tell me why my father had to die!" "Tell me why bad things happen to decent people."

Nobody can do it. No one has all the knowledge, all the insight. We become justifiably angry when people try to give easy and incomplete answers to the question of our pain. In the long run, you and I don't want to be told why difficult things in our lives are as they are. The purpose of our pain is, I think, something we must figure out for ourselves.

GREAT EXPECTATIONS

Our doorbell rang late on a November evening. Since my wife was working in the kitchen, I closed its door as I responded to the summons.

I did my best to be a responsible host. Opening the front door with one hand, I touched the light-switch with the other. The switch was up, and I supposed the lights were on.

Please remember I am totally blind. The condition surely creates interesting circumstances.

Nan was standing on the porch. She needed to talk, and I ushered her into the living room. We visited quite a while and then prayed. Finally, I accompanied Nan to the door and wished her a cheery good-night.

As I returned to our kitchen, my wife asked about the company. Glancing into the living room she said, "You did turn the lights on for her, didn't you?"

Thunder-struck, I said I had checked and found the switch up. Mary Evelyn then reminded me our front room lights were on a three-way switch. The room had, in fact, been totally dark all the time Nan and I were visiting.

And Nan hadn't said a single word about it! I suspect she gained a new appreciation of darkness that evening.

At first blush, complete darkness is shocking, and even frightening. After a person has been in it for a while, though, he or she becomes more or less used to the lack of light.

In earlier chapters, we, along with Mr. Job, struggled to gain a deeper understanding of human suffering. We discovered many elements of truth, but were repeatedly frustrated and disappointed. In effect we found ourselves living in a sort of intellectual and spiritual darkness. We have profound questions which seem to defy common-sense and reason.

In this chapter we will take a few moments to look deeply into ourselves and examine some of the basic notions and suppositions that drive us. Perhaps this examination will open doors for us to have clearer understanding.

Humankind, from the time of Adam until the dawn of our own age, has taken pain, suffering, and death for granted. Such things were part of life, and folks expected them as everyday occurrences.

I am staggered by thoughts of medicine in former generations. What did people do when surgery was unknown and there was a ruptured appendix? How were common infections dealt with before the day of modern drugs?

When my childhood friend, Bobby, had blood-poisoning he teetered for many days on the brink between life and death. This was in the 1940's when modern medicine was already coming of age. How must it have been for sufferers of former decades and centuries?

Back in 1950, Charlie and his brother, Jack, each came down with polio. Both boys were consigned to iron-lungs. These huge machines breathed for them and labored to keep them alive.

Jack died while lying beside his stricken brother. Charlie couldn't move a hand to wipe tears from his eyes or wave Jack good-bye. I knew those boys. They were my friends.

We all have memories of where we were and what we were doing when certain things happened. When F.D.R. died, I was a nine-year-old kid listening to "Hop Harrigan" on our living room radio. When J.F.K. was shot, I was in the upstairs study of our parsonage in Terhune, Indiana.

Well, when the announcement of Dr. Salk's vaccine for polio was made, I was in a car and on my way to lunch at our fraternity house. It was a sunny, October day, and we were turning from West Hampton Drive and heading south towards 42nd Street. I was deeply moved as the fantastic news came in on the car radio.

Before that time in 1954, polio was a profoundly dreaded disease. As a matter of fact, prior to this century, a host of ailments and illnesses were perpetual threats to the lives of our forefathers and foremothers.

Think of the hardy men and women who came on horseback, rode in covered wagons, poled their way down rivers, and walked on aching feet from one coast of this continent to the other. Life was hard for them. Death was an ever-present companion.

Go back through the centuries, and remember life as it was lived in Bible days. Wild animals prowled hills and waited to pounce on unsuspecting victims. Enemy tribes were on the move, ready to kill or be killed.

Vast expanses of the Bible-lands were desert and received only one or two inches of rain in an entire year. Even in "the land of milk and honey," food was in short and very undependable supply.

Listen to these words of the Psalmist: "He will deliver you from the snare of the fowler and from the deadly pestilence; He will cover you with His pinions, and under His wings you will find refuge; His faithfulness is a shield and buckler. You will not fear the terror of the night, nor the arrow that flies by day, nor the pestilence that stalks in darkness, nor the destruction that waits at noonday. A thousand may fall at your side, ten thousand at your right hand; but it will not come near you. You will only look with your eyes and see the recompense of the wicked."

"Because you have made the Lord your refuge, the Most High your habitation, no evil shall befall you, no scourge come near your tent. For He will give His angels charge of you to guard you in all your ways." (Psalm 91:3-11)

In these verses, and in countless other places, the writer of Psalms took the troubles of this world totally for granted. He sometimes wondered why the wicked prospered while God's people were heaped with afflictions, but the fact of suffering and pain was a thing he simply accepted.

The Psalmist did not ask, "Why?" Instead he declared God to be the source of help in all sorts of difficulty.

I remember preaching Eugene's funeral. The young man, a member of my church, had died in a fox-hole in Vietnam. Ten agonizing days passed between the time his parents received the terrible telegram and the day his body was returned for burial.

For my funeral text, I chose opening lines from the 46th Psalm. "God is our refuge and strength, a very present help in trouble." (Psalm 46:1)

"Our lives are packed with problems and troubles," I said. "God promises His people strength to successfully meet the challenge of every difficulty."

Let's consider other expectations of life held by men and women of earlier years. These were folks who knew the horrendous heat of summer and biting cold of winter. They had neither air conditioning nor central heating. They took nature as it was and were grateful for warmth generated by a small fire or a tree's shade.

45

The point is this. People of former centuries expected things to be tough and weren't a bit surprised when they turned out that way. With us of the late twentieth century, it is a different matter.

I sit in our kitchen and consider its numerous conveniences. Among them are the range — complete with oven and timers — and the frost-free refrigerator-freezer. Also on hand and ready for service are the dishwasher, disposal, microwave, toaster, mixer, and coffee-maker. A television and VCR stand on the counter waiting to entertain us while food is prepared or consumed.

Ours is not an unusually plush kitchen. It contains equipment common to homes across the land.

Comfortable and convenient as our kitchen may be, I arrive home in the evening to hear my wife say, "Honey, let's eat out tonight." I respond to her suggestion, "Oh, why don't we eat at home? We'll send out for pizza."

A replica of the Mayflower awaits tourists at Plymouth, Massachusetts. The ship was built in the 1950s and sailed from England to the place where it is now anchored.

I have paid admission and visited the Mayflower on two different occasions. Each time I was impressed by incredibly cramped conditions. A sign posted on the boat says it is authentic in most respects. A few inches, however, have been added to the between decks head-room so as to accommodate today's tourists.

A few inches added? I stretch to five feet eight inches, and I can barely walk in that lower deck area without bowing or banging my head!

I compare the Mayflower to the 747 on which we flew to Israel. The trip was made in a comfort-controlled cabin. We were served fine meals, entertained with a recent movie, and pampered in every conceivable way.

Early pilgrims were seasick for miserable weeks, and we traversed a far greater distance in mere hours. At the flight's end, a few of us grumbled about having to sit still so long.

Psychologists say ours is the first generation of humans whose first concern is anything other than survival. In former times, and in other parts of today's world, men and women spend their lives scratching for food, guarding themselves against enemies, and living in fear of disease.

People of our time and place dwell in security to the point our primary quest is one of life's meaning. "Is my life worth anything?" That's what we want to know. We fill counselors' offices and couches in the attempt to understand and justify our existence.

Young people stood in the front of my church and sang. Their song had one of those ambiguous tunes which wander around and don't seem to get anywhere.

Their words, though, caught my attention. "Is there a place for us?" The question frequently repeated itself and was always sung with intensity.

That's what kids want to know. "Is there a place for us — for me?"

The U.S. Declaration Of Independence has set the tone of our time. We all remember its assertion that among humankind's inalienable rights are "life, liberty, and the pursuit of happiness."

Somehow, we've lost the words "pursuit of" from our way of thinking. "I have a right to be happy," person after frustrated person declares. "I have a right. . ."

There is a strange contradiction in the ways we experience and understand affairs of our days. A profound cynicism overlies our corporate life. We don't trust political leaders, and we are generally convinced "Murphy's Law" is on target.

We seem to separate political happenings from personal well-being. Perhaps we are helped by the semi-reality of television. We are, in fact, so satiated by TV news that it merges in our minds with all the thrillers and who-done-its which fill the screen.

For one reason or another, our generation does not think in personal terms about the frequently tragic happenings reported either in print or on the tube. In so far as individual lives are concerned, we expect everything to be okay. We simply can't understand it when a thirteen-year-old friend comes down with cancer or a neighbor's toddler is run over in the street.

"What's going on?" We throw up our hands in frustration. "This isn't fair," we say. "Why do things like that happen anyhow?"

Our changed expectations of life, have, then, filled us with a new battery of questions and concerns. They have, in fact, given us an entirely different perspective of the world.

When our grandparents expected life to be tough, they weren't surprised or frustrated to find it so. The more comfortable our lives have become, the more shocked and perplexed we are when tough reality continues to come our way.

I think of Steve. As a teenager, this splendid, young man accompanied a work-team to Haiti. The young people worked in a variety of places which included Grace Children's Hospital — a facility for tubercular kids.

Steve, from a middle-class American home, could not believe or accept the poverty he saw. He was personally crushed by the death of a Haitian infant whom he had held in his arms. Steve came home a changed person.

It could have gone either way, but for Steve the change was devastating. He could not believe such horror could exist in a world made by the good God. Steve didn't formally renounce his faith; his relationship with the Church simply faded and died.

A Jewish friend says many of his people had similar feelings as the news of Hitler's Holocaust spread around the world. "We know evil exists," they said, "but this is too much!" To many of them, the idea of God being good became a bitter joke.

Arnold and his wife, Betty, were members of one of my first congregations. I was told they hadn't attended services for years, and I took them on as a personal challenge.

Calling at Arnold's home, I found this man to be a Biblically literate person who understood a great deal of theology. I couldn't imagine why he and his wife weren't in worship and Sunday School. Then I heard their personal story.

Arnold and Betty had been blessed with a beautiful daughter who was the light of their lives. When the child was eight years old, she became terribly ill.

Arnold prayed, prayed, and prayed for his daughter. He firmly believed God would answer his prayers and was shaken to his soul's foundations when the little girl died.

Was God not faithful, or were Arnold's prayers not offered properly? The man batted terrible questions back and forth through his heart, soul, and mind. He stopped coming to worship. Something wasn't right, and Arnold simply slipped beyond the boundaries of the congregation.

Inaccurate and unfounded expectations can get folks in big trouble. If we look for something that doesn't turn out to be real, we simply don't know what to do.

So let's not kid ourselves. Illnesses happen; accidents are a part of life; and every one of us will, sooner or later, come to death.

Life has toughness in it. We can be grateful for agricultural, medical, and social advances, but these gains don't, for a moment, change the nature of the world which we inhabit.

I heard a well-respected doctor talking about recent medical advances. He spoke of antibiotics, new victories in the battle against heart-disease, and many other medical accomplishments. He went on to anticipate a victory over cancer.

Maybe the devil made me do it, but when the doctor finished his presentation and asked for questions, I raised a hand and asked, "If we conquer all these medical challenges, how, then, will we die?"

There was nervous laughter in the room. The doctor spoke a few meaningless words and turned to the next question.

Folks, we are going to die. Things are going to go wrong in our lives. These are simple facts we must accept if we are to have any adequate appreciation of who we are.

Great expectations are wonderful, but if they are not congruent with reality, they will get us in lots of hot water. Honest expectations can, on the other hand, enable us to understand and appreciate life as it is intended to be lived.

Do you say I haven't solved the problem at all? Have I simply declared illness, pain, and death to be real in our world?

You're right, but remember, excessive expecting can get us in big trouble. Let's hold on to the thought and turn another page.

IN ALL THINGS

"If life hands you a lemon, make lemonade." The phrase is overly used and excessively simplistic. It does, however, help us round a mental corner and view pains and problems from a fresh perspective.

Until now we have been asking why people suffer. Underlying the question is an assumption that there must be a reason. We have searched the mind of God and affairs of humankind and haven't found it. Let's change our thinking and approach the question from an entirely different angle.

We can rack souls, strain minds, and talk ourselves blue in the face in an effort to discover why affairs of our lives are as they are. Let's, for the moment, simply accept these affairs as realities.

We must begin with these realities and go on to examine them in a very intentional way. Perhaps we can discover the value and meaning which they invariably harbor.

Consider past president Ronald Reagan. In November, 1994, Mr. Reagan disclosed a medical diagnosis that he suffered from Alzheimer's disease. In almost the next breath, our former president said he hoped his illness would open the way for people to have a deeper and more humane view of Alzheimer's.

In an earlier chapter, I wrote of a young man named Eugene. He died years ago while serving as a U.S. Marine in Vietnam.

Eugene's parents were uneasy about the war in which he had given his life. The night before the funeral, we talked at length about the meaning and value of his death.

These parents needed to discover, or create, some sense of purpose in their son's tragic death. They later presented a beautiful memorial display-case to our church and were largely responsible for a Vietnam Veterans' Memorial on the grounds of the local high school.

They needed a sign that Eugene's life would be remembered, that it had value in the fleeting affairs of the world. They, in effect, made lemonade.

I, personally, could tell a similar story. I would not, for a minute, say that God struck me with blindness so as to put me through the mill of tough experiences and create a better pastor. My blindness is something that happened. Perhaps it was hereditary; perhaps it came from an unusual collision of genes.

The simple fact is that I lost my sight. My life was shaped by a series of toughening circumstances, and I became a better pastor than I would otherwise have been.

In the eighth chapter of Romans, and in my favorite translations of it, Paul wrote: "We know that in all things God works for the good of those who love Him, who have been called according to His purpose." (Romans 8:28 N.I.V.)

Please contrast this rendering of the text with the one found in the King James Version and some other translations. "We know that all things work together for good to them that love God, to them who are the called according to His purpose." (Romans 8:28 K.J.V.)

At first blush these two translated verses seem more or less the same. They aren't. The "in all things" text opens a new door for us to understand God's activity in our lives. The "all things work" version tends to bottle us up in a highly constricted world.

I am not a student of Greek and am no authority on Paul's linguistics. I am a student of life and of God. The distinction between renderings of Romans 8:28 is something I find soul-wrenching.

In the traditional version, printed in the King James and many other Bible translations, Paul says that "all things work together for good. . ." The words imply that affairs of human activity, elemental forces of nature, and the course of history all conspire to create good for God's people.

This way of thinking pushes us to ask the question, "Why?" Surely there is an answer; all we need to do is find it!

The other translation, however, tells us that "in all things God works for good. . ." The implication here is that events of our lives may be random or even negative. Alzheimer's, AIDS, auto accidents, and earthquakes may, in themselves, be bad, but God enters the fray to help his sons and daughters bring good out of them.

Human freedom is one cornerstone of "in all things" thinking. God has given us the ability to make decisions and have governing control of our lives. This being so, we can not hold to the notion that "all things work together for good."

I have the freedom to decide I will take a walk uptown. The person driving in my general direction has been given the same freedom to decide how many beers he will consume. That driver's decision may well have an impact on my life. In other words, neither I, nor the God who made me, has control of all events which come my way.

In previous centuries, devoted Christians fought terrible battles over the question of predestination. History tells us men were even burnt at the stake because they did not believe "properly" on this issue.

Frankly, predestination isn't a very hot conversation topic, even among clergy, in today's society. We have largely discarded the doctrine and laid it aside.

In a secular way, though, predestination is still with us. It is called "determinism," and it is part of who we are.

The fourth grader came home from school with a straight F report card. Not wanting to be the recipient of parental anger, he beat Mom and Dad to the punch. "Well, folks," he asked, "what do you put it up to — environment or heredity?"

We, who are scientifically oriented, tend to think in causal terms. We ask, "Why did you do something or other," and expect a reasonable answer. Is it any wonder our kids have a stock and exasperating response: "Because."

If it were completely possible for us to spell out specific reasons why we do the things we do, there would be little, if any, freedom left in the human equation. The fact is we do things "because" — because we choose to do them.

It's nice to pass the buck. If we can say, "He made me do it," or "I just didn't have any choice," we seem to get ourselves off the hook of responsibility.

And, of course, there are all sorts of events and conditions which do affect our actions and nudge us in one direction or the other. Let's remind ourselves that we are free and accountable. It's not fair to try passing the buck on to anyone, especially not to God.

And, if we are free and responsible for our own lives, others are also. This entire world, then, is composed of people who function with personal freedom. Because of this shared freedom, no one can reasonably say that God is in charge of all things.

It's tough to admit it. Contrary to popular view, God's will is not always done.

I've been a pastor long enough to be a firm believer in sin. Men and women frequently make lousy and damaging decisions. God allows us this ability and, with it, He has surrendered His control over all our affairs.

So I am free; you are free; we all are free to make choices. The decisions we make have interacting effects. I sometimes suffer because of your mistakes, and you for mine. I can not contend that "all things" are designed to work together for good, because all things are not even in the mind and controlling hand of God.

Here's another cornerstone for "in all things" thinking. Much sin and pain must be viewed socially and not personally.

Back in the mid-'80s, when AIDS first came into public consciousness, a prominent television evangelist declared victims of the disease to be suffering for their sins. He referred to deviant sexual behavior and irresponsible use of drugs as the twin causes of AIDS. He said the illness was God's judgement upon persons who had flagrantly misbehaved.

At the time this was going on, I was pastoring a congregation near Kokomo, Indiana. Folks in our community were all aware of young Ryan White who was an AIDS victim through a blood transfusion.

There was a tremendous argument among parents of children attending Ryan's school. Many did not want the boy admitted to classes and school activities. Not knowing much about AIDS, they feared young Ryan would pass the illness along to their sons and daughters.

Current evidence tells us these parents were driven by unfounded fears. Back then, though, available information cast a far less clear picture.

In the midst of their arguing, no one suggested that Ryan White was suffering for his sins. It was painfully clear to all that this fine boy was a victim of sinful circumstances.

Irresponsible sexual behavior and use of drugs may, in fact, give life to the AIDS virus. In this sense the illness can be seen as judgement upon a society which behaves in such a way.

The judgement, however, is on society. Lots of individuals suffer because of the sinful activity of others. They are caught between grind-stones of circumstance.

There is nothing new with such a thought. A father gets drunk and beats his daughter. The little girl hasn't done a thing to deserve her pain.

A war begins, and its bombs and bullets take lives of the innocent. How can we possibly say these people got what they had coming to them?

And what about Mrs. Job? The Bible-writer, Mr. Job and his friends, and uncounted generations of wondering men and women have pulled spiritual hair in the attempt to understand why the poor fellow suffered. What about his wife?

Mrs. Job also was deprived of home, family, and comfort. She wasn't afflicted with illness, but she had a heavy burden of care for someone who was. How must she have felt?

Loved ones, companions, and care-givers around the world surely empathize with Mrs. Job. They have been shouldered with personal sacrifice and stress of all descriptions. For the most part, they are innocent side-kicks whose suffering is tremendously great.

"In all things" God works for His people's good. In the midst of sin, pain, swirling, and life-threatening circumstance, God is at our side helping and enabling us to find positive results.

The Psalmist wrote, "Even though I walk through the valley of the shadow of death, I shall fear no evil, for Thou art with me. . ." (Psalm 23:4) The dark valley was, to him, very real. God's accompanying grace was even more evident.

A parable is told by those acquainted with the art of Oriental Rug making. According to it, the master weaver is stationed at one side of the loom while his apprentices are on the other. The weaver gives his protégés a chart telling what strands should be pushed through which holes. They must collaborate with the weaver in pushing the threads back and forth and creating the rug.

It is the master weaver's job to take strands passed through to him and tie them into the pattern. Even when an apprentice blunders and sends through the wrong strand, the weaver must accept and use it. In effect, he constantly recreates the pattern so as to include and accommodate his apprentices' mistakes.

God is like that. He labors with us in dynamic moments of experience. He accepts the many strands of life thrust at Him and knows some are according to His pattern while others are not. It is as if He works with us and says, "Okay friends, under the circumstances where do we go from here?"

You and I may never know why things happen to us. The "why" may, in fact, simply be that we were in the right place at the wrong time. There may be no profound and eternal reason for the mountain of circumstances heaped upon us.

We can, however, find a sense of purpose in them. God works with us in this regard. He collaborates in helping us find and bring positive consequences to our happenings and affairs.

We sit around a table and talk. To say the least, our group is diverse. Harold and I are blind; Joe, Marty, and Susan are hearing impaired; and David, who suffers from M.S. is wheelchair bound.

There are others in the group. Betty and Sherry, grand souls that they are, are with us because of shared concern. We are our annual conference's Disabilities In Ministry Committee.

Our group strives to raise the consciousness level among United Methodist congregations in northern Indiana. We have written two general publications and created a thirteen week Sunday School course, interpreting disabilities and the disabled to folks who live "ordinary" lives.

Our group has been together for several years. We have a huge task. Creating a major shift in the way congregations think and do things is akin to moving mountains.

I have deep sympathy for the churches. Many congregations are housed in buildings which were constructed in a different era. The structures include lots of steps, narrow halls, and hard to access rest rooms. The cost for updating these facilities so as to make them "handicapped-accessible" is astronomical.

These churches must be encouraged to do things that are possible for them. Right now, and at very little cost, they can produce large-print worship bulletins, and also have large-print Bibles, hymnals, devotional materials, and Church School literature. Hearing-assist equipment is also relatively inexpensive. If the churches only have a will, they will find the way to make many improvements for the benefit of physically and mentally limited people.

In responding to a recent questionnaire, church after church said they encouraged disabled people to assume leadership in their worship services. On the same sheet of paper, the congregations indicated they didn't have ramps to elevated levels of chancels and choir lofts.

Our committee is studying these questionnaires and responding to them with encouraging notes. We try to be gentle in telling congregations they can't have it both ways. The fact is that if they want disabled people helping with liturgical leadership, and if they even want them attending worship and other activities, they must make it physically possible for these folks to get in the doors and up the steps.

But we are discussing the committee itself. Most of us are what the world calls "handicapped." We are, in fact, using our limitations as tools of ministry to others.

God works with us. He helps us transform a variety of very difficult personal problems into positive means for ministry. "In all things" He works for our good.

Now, here's a cautioning word. The "in all things" point of view is something each person has to figure out for himself. If some well-meaning soul tries to do it for us, he's in danger of having his scalp lifted. I can't make such an interpretation for you, and you can't do it for me.

I don't want a well-intending character telling me I should be glad because I'm blind and God will use my lack of sight as a benefit. My friend, David, doesn't need to be told he should be thrilled to be in a wheelchair.

Please don't try to tell us why the painful components of our lives can have good consequences. Be patient, and let us work it out for ourselves. Similarly, we must allow you opportunity to make your own discoveries.

I commenced this chapter by quoting a cliche: "If life hands you a lemon, make lemonade." I close it with the same prescription.

It is more than a psychological game. It is more than putting a good face on a bad situation. "Making lemonade" is a positive facing of life's circumstances and the conviction God is facing them with us.

Meeting us in the dynamic present is God's way of relating to His sons and daughters. He meets us in life's converging affairs and says, "Well, where do we go from here?"

Pastor Steve is not only a minister, he is an ardent outdoorsman and hunter. He tells of a recent day when a farmer in his congregation phoned him.

"Get out here right away. I really have something to show you."

When Pastor Steve arrived at the scene, he was taken to the middle of a corn field. There he was shown two buck deer who had died with antlers locked together.

Whether the deer killed each other in combat, or starved because of their inability to separate, is a question in dispute. One way or the other, they locked horns and died in the process.

Steve now has these deer-heads stuffed and mounted. They are in his home, a silent witness to the thing which happens when antlers are stubbornly locked.

You and I can perpetually debate the causes and reasons for human suffering. We can also give up the strength of our lives while locked in such continued questioning.

There comes a time to simply go ahead with life. We must remember that "in all things" God works for our good.

The lemons of our lives can be very bitter. God's is the sweetness which turns them into lemonade.

SIMPLE TRUTH

"Emerson, honey, you'd better call an ambulance. I think I'm having a heart attack."

Roberta's words were spoken with a calm voice. As a matter of fact, she has pronounced them several times during the last three decades. What's more, she has been right in every instance.

Asked about her tranquility in moments of crisis, Roberta gives a simple response. "I believe I have the best doctors in the area. I trust them completely. Someday they won't be able to bring me back, and that's okay too. My God is good."

In this book's several pages, you and I have discussed many matters. We have talked of countless interacting forces which affect the course of our lives. We have tried to study various strands of complex truth. Now we come to something that's not at all complex. "God is good." It's as simple as that.

Simple truth is hard to find these days. When my wife asks me what I want for supper I say, "It depends." I go ahead to explore a variety of alternatives.

I want to know if we are eating in or out, early or late; with friends or by ourselves. If we are dining at home, I want to know what is in the refrigerator and freezer; if out, how much money is in our wallets.

A seemingly simple decision is really quite complicated. I need lots of information before speaking of my tummy's desires.

Life is like that. In our day its complexity has multiplied again and again.

The computer on which I write is a case in point. My particular model is equipped with a speech-synthesizer that talks along with my typing and reads everything back to me. This computer has become an essential part of who I am.

Back when I was a kid, home typewriters were unusual. Now we live with computers and a strange new language of hardware, software, hertz, hard-drives, RAM capacity, and modems.

Posters found in many of today's offices tell the story of our time. "If you think everything is okay, it's obvious you don't understand the situation."

Well, life isn't simple. Human knowledge has exploded since the mid-part of this century, and its rate of increase constantly escalates.

We don't really like things this way, for something deep inside us calls for simple answers. Such simplicity is hard to find.

Amish folk live near my northern Indiana community. Their horse-drawn buggies roll regularly past our door. When we drive into the country, we see these folks attempting to live their "simple" style of life.

They have a tough time doing it. As we pass one Amish farm, we see a pay-phone standing beside the corn field. These people won't have a telephone in their houses, but they can't get along without one in their lives.

Quite a few Amish work in local industries. Some come to the job on bicycle or in buggy. Many others, though, leave horse and buggy behind and hire people with vans for transportation to and from the shop.

I write these words with great compassion. I appreciate the yearning for a former and simpler day. I wouldn't mind a little of that life myself. The fact is, though, that we don't live in a simple world.

Young people are frequently commended for their idealism. They can become wonderfully passionate in backing a political cause, or religious persuasion.

I suspect youth are not so much idealistic as simplistic. They want to have uncomplicated solutions to terribly complex problems.

The Bible seems to offer simple answers, and we sophisticates who live near the beginning of the twenty-first century are often leery of them. My mother, for instance, had absolutely no tolerance for the closing section of Job.

You remember the flow of the story. Job is afflicted with a multitude of problems; he struggles to understand his pain and difficulties; he finally says, "Lord, you're God;" and at the end he is rewarded.

Job is given back his land, returned to wealth, and presented with a new crop of beautiful children. He lives happily ever after, or at least until he dies at a ripe, old age.

It was the part of the story having to do with children which really got to my mother. She insisted that no child can ever make up for the loss of another.

Mom had a right to speak out on the subject. Her oldest son, my brother — Dale, was killed in an auto accident when he was twenty-two years old. Absolutely nothing and no one could fill the empty place Dale's death left in my mother's heart.

She was right. Saying Mr. Job had everything come out okay in the end, was an inadequate way of concluding the story. It was, however, the best avenue open to Job's author.

"The Lord is good. His steadfast love endures forever, and His faithfulness to all generations." (Psalm 100:8) This affirmation appears repeatedly in the Psalms and throughout the entire Bible. Divine goodness is at the heart of virtually all Biblical thinking.

Deep in our hearts, you and I all know God's goodness is an item of belief. People attempt to prove it by pointing to the beauty of a spring day, the fragrance of a rose, the innocence of a new-born child, and the taste of good food. They view the world selectively and speak of God's benevolence.

Throughout these pages, we have discussed various forms of pain, hurt, and evil. We know them well, and experience them nearly as often as we do the good things. Those of us who view life objectively can summon as much evidence for Divine malice as we can mercy.

But the Lord is good. At the core of creation, when complex layers of pain and heart-break are peeled away, God works in our behalf. This is a basic article of faith and is the truth upon which we base our days and nights.

Barbara knew it. This woman experienced more pain than would have been right for an entire community. She suffered from diabetes and a host of associated diseases. Her younger son came into the world with multiple birth-defects. He had undergone nearly fifty surgeries before his tenth birthday.

As death approached, Barbara was hospitalized again. In her forties, she was experiencing great discomfort.

"Barbara," a visiting friend inquired, "how can you possibly believe in God when you suffer like this?"

The answer was immediate. "I couldn't possibly endure these sufferings if I didn't believe in Him!"

Barbara died on Easter Sunday. The twin accounts of death and resurrection were the essence of her life-story. And Barbara was convinced God is good.

We can not prove either Divine goodness or maliciousness. That God is good is a simple act of believing. It is the hub upon which the days of our lives rotate.

Ultimately we speak of the resurrection of Jesus. In it is conclusive evidence of God's victory in our behalf. The resurrection is, in fact, at the center of our Christian being.

But we speak of more than "pie in the sky by and by." God, who is with us in the critical present, helps us discover and bring out good from whatever comes our way. When we think of His activity in our behalf, we speak of what He is doing every bit as much as what He has done.

This book tells the story of Mr. Job. In one sense it speaks of the Biblical Job. In another, I find myself puffing my way through life in Mr. Job's shoes. More importantly, you who read these pages may be casting yourself as the title character.

Hard to understand circumstances eventually come to every one of us. Illness, pain, accident, and death must, sooner or later, cast heavy shadows upon our lives.

Throwing up our hands and asking, "Why?" isn't really very productive. Sometimes our questioning word is no more than a child-like attempt to argue matters of injustice with the One who has made us. Never do we find answers that really satisfy.

Perhaps it helps a little to pause and realize that our frustrations often rise from false expectations. The more fanciful our expectations are, the more we are likely to be disappointed by them.

Finally, though, we find peace in recognizing that, in the midst of apparent evil, God works to help us find good in our days. In the last analysis, we bow souls before Him and trust His goodness.

God is good! Mr. Job, it's as simple as that!

A PERSONAL POSTSCRIPT

Time moves on. Nearly three years have passed since I turned off my computer with the belief this small book was written and ready for publication. Then the clock ticked another tock, and now I am writing again.

In the forgoing chapters I made repeated reference to pain in my back and leg. It began several months earlier and deviled me for the better part of a year.

My pain was quite similar to one I had known seven years earlier. At that time I required back surgery. My family doctor and I both supposed the most recent problem was a reoccurrence of my 1988 ailment.

On March 2, 1995, I traveled to a South Bend hospital for a myelogram. Physical therapy and exercises of all sorts hadn't lessened personal discomfort, and my physician wanted to know exactly what was going on within me.

Well, the myelogram was immediately followed with a CT- scan. I lay on the table and was pushed into a tunnel-like machine. It ground and shifted for a while, and I was variously told to breathe deeply and hold my breath.

Finally all pictures were taken. I lay there, waiting for instructions to climb down and prepare for the journey home.

"I don't want to frighten you, sir," a nurse said, "but we want to take more pictures. We believe we've found a mass in the lower, right-hand part of your body."

That moment marked the beginning of a continuing series of CT-scans, biopsies, surgeries and radiation treatments. The growth turned out to be cancerous, and I have been trying to learn how "to live" with it.

In March there was a needle biopsy which was followed by two operations. In May my wife and I drove to Rochester, Minnesota's Mayo Clinic in search of the best possible medical advice.

"This isn't what you want to hear," the Mayo doctor said, "but the tumor is still inside you, and it's growing. You'll have to have more surgery and treatment."

It wasn't what I wanted to hear. The weakening of my right leg, and pain which shrieks through it, weren't what I wanted to feel either. All at once, this sixty-year-old pastor was in very serious medical trouble and on almost everyone's prayer-list.

Summer 1995 found me undergoing radiation treatments, and in August I returned to Mayo's for "chain-saw" surgery. That's what one of the doctors called it. He pulled no punches.

In a lengthy operation, the surgeon had cut out, scraped away, and otherwise removed every evidence of cancer he could find. Before my incision was closed, all of the surgical fields were "sprayed" with interoperative radiation.

Mayo doctors were concerned because they had to cut a major nerve running into my leg. The cancer had encircled it to the point the nerve had to go if the growth was to be removed.

Now, as I continue with my life, I wait to discover what will happen within me. The surgeon pronounced himself 80 to 90% sure my growth would not reappear in the old areas. He warned me, however, it could come back in other places.

I'm getting along better than folks thought I could. Doctors and nurses were afraid that, after the operation, I might not be able to walk. As a matter of fact, I use a cane these days, and my gait isn't swift. The pain is gone, though, and I really get around pretty well.

I will always remember the first shower I took in the hospital. The nurse was so concerned about my ability to stand that she nearly climbed into the tub with me. She didn't want to get her uniform soaked, though, and I was finally able to give myself a great watering down.

Years have now passed, and I can only guess about the future. I hope for good years to come and realize I may not die of old age. For the time being, however, I have life, and I want to take full advantage of each moment.

"Here we go again," a voice inside me has been crying. "Ralph, it's like your going blind or experiencing hearing loss. 'Same song, second verse, a little bit louder, a little bit worse!'"

If I may quote a well-known baseball philosopher, "It ain't over until it's over." You and I must never assume we have met and conquered all life's challenges and that there will be no more of them before us. Our days and nights flow in inexorable pulsation.

The specific challenges we face change as we pass through life's various ages and stages. When I was a boy I struggled to ride a bike without skinning a knee or breaking my neck. A few years later, my problems were those imposed by puberty. Then there were marriage, parenthood, and my life's work. All the time there have been issues of health and well being.

The continuing struggle can actually bring deep satisfaction. Successfully meeting and resolving life's challenges can, in fact, evoke an orgasmic quality of joy. The challenges keep coming, and they will do so at least until the day we die.

A theology professor I once knew declared his belief in perpetual purgatory. He insisted that growth is the source of all joy and that a place of eternal bliss would be boring and uninteresting.

I read back over these lines and can scarcely credit my senses. I am, in fact, declaring cancer and death to be part of my continuing and eternal adventure.

In earlier years I have met other challenges, and some of them have been pretty tough. One of these days I will discover the degree to which I can die faithfully and triumphantly.

During Lent of 1995, I was hospitalized for my initial surgeries. At that time I was scheduled to preach a series of sermons on "The Last Words Of Jesus Of Nazareth." As I lay in a hospital bed, and later experienced weeks of home-bound recuperation, I canceled one message after another. I kept working these sermons around in my mind, though, and found myself comparing Jesus' last words with my own thoughts and feelings.

Christ's words from the cross fall into three categories. First, He expressed physical need and emotional anguish: "'I Thirst,'" and "'My God, why hast Thou forsaken me?'" (John 19:28 and Matthew 27:46)

Again, Jesus was concerned for those about Him: "'Behold your son — your mother,' " He said to John and Mary. (John 19:26-27) In another breath, He told a fellow victim of crucifixion, "'Today, you will be with me in paradise.'" (Luke 23:43)

Ultimately, Christ faithfully entrusted Himself into the hands of Eternal Grace. "'It is finished.'" "'Into Thy hands I commit My spirit.'" (John 19:30 and Luke 23:46)

Well, I know and have felt all of the above. I, for instance, have experienced pain and grumbled about it with great frequency. I have also known time when I have lain in bed and cried until my spirit was drained.

There is much I still want to do. My soul screams at the very thought of leaving wife, daughter, and grandchildren. I know they would be able to take care of themselves; I also know the same Grace which has brought me through the years would watch over them. I know these things, but am still in no rush to leave them.

Caring for my family was an immediate concern. Even before my Mayo operation, Mary Evelyn and I went houseshopping. We have now moved from the church's parsonage and into our single-story, retirement home. There are no more steps to climb!

In the United Methodist Church an active, pastoral family is comfortably housed. The day a minister retires, though, or a few weeks after his wife is left a widow, that sweet story is over. The parsonage must be vacated to make room for a new ministerial family.

In the summer of 1995, I had no way of knowing if I would make it until retirement, be forced to leave ministry because of disability, or simply die with pastoral boots on. Whatever the eventuality, either Mary Evelyn and I, or my wife by herself, would have had to acquire personally owned walls and roof. I wanted to help her with the decisions and choices. Doing so brought me deep satisfaction.

In like manner, I addressed our congregation and offered it my family. "Behold your sister, your daughter, your grandchildren," I said. "Care for them well."

Writing these words was very difficult. I struggled with tears even while sitting at my desk and typing.

The typing was important. Completing and publishing this book has filled me with a sense of urgency. Issues of Divine goodness and human suffering have always been close to my heart. I have now been driven to make this statement of analysis and faith.

Ultimately, God is in charge of all things. I rejoice in life and am not afraid of death. The Lord is good, and His mercy certainly extends to the grave and beyond.

Some folks live in perpetual uncertainty regarding their salvation. "Will I go to heaven when I die?" is their unending question.

Christian friends, we need have no doubts in this regard. Eternal mercy comes to us, not because we are good enough to merit it, but because He is so gracious as to give it. God is, indeed, good.

Many Americans found the Spring of 1995 to be especially difficult. On April 19 — only three days after Easter — the federal building in Oklahoma City was destroyed by a massive bomb blast. Over 160 lives were taken, and grief shrouded the nation.

The old questions were raised: How can such things happen? What did all those people do to deserve the pain, anguish and death which came their way?

Well, Oklahoma City's First United Methodist Church stood close to that federal building, and it too was damaged.

Walls were blown out, doors were torn from their hinges, and stained glass windows were shattered.

Soon after the blast, the church's pastor and an Oklahoma City detective entered the building and surveyed the damage. Beyond the rubble they saw an amazing thing.

On the sanctuary's sagging balcony railing, stood Easter lilies from the previous Sunday. All displayed their blooms. Not a one had been toppled from its perch.

It was a sign of resurrection in the midst of death and destruction. It is a reminder that God's grace will always survive and surpass whatever pain this world can serve us.

"Eat this bread; it is Christ to you." I was bathed in Judean sunshine as I spoke the words. Along with others in our travel-group, I stood in a Jerusalem garden. With an olive-wood cup in hand, I then said, "Drink the cup; it is Christ to you."

These lines describe a high moment in my pastoral life. The Communion service I celebrated was only yards away from an empty first-century tomb. Many believe it to be the site of Jesus' burial and resurrection.

There are, in Israel, two possible locations for Christ's death, burial, and resurrection. A large church - The Church Of The Holy Sepulchre — stands over one of them. The garden in which we communed is the other.

Frankly, I'm not enough of an archaeologist to make any judgement concerning the sites' authenticity. In so far as personal devotion is concerned, though, I have very positive feelings about the Garden Tomb.

On a hillside above that tomb is a strange configuration of rocks. It has the likeness of a skull. The New Testament tells us Jesus was crucified at "Golgotha (which means the place of the skull)." (Matthew 27:33)

A first-century olive press was found near the tomb. It strongly suggests that a garden of olive trees grew here in Christ's time.

Whether we were, or were not, at the actual place of the resurrection is a little beside the point. In my own soul I felt myself to be in the Easter garden, and I was sharing Holy Communion with friends. It was a rare and wonderful moment, and it came only days before the onset of my current adventure with cancer.

Now I glance back over the pages of this Postscript and realize I have said nothing new. These paragraphs constitute a chapter in the account of my personal pilgrimage that does nothing more than repeat and ratify all that has been said before it.

During the circling of years, we have painful experiences which defy all attempts of explanation. Accepting them is important. Discovering the presence of God working beside us in bringing good out of evil and joy out of pain is certainly a source of profound satisfaction.

In the last analysis, though, we simply renew our trust in the One who has made us and who loves us. Surely the Psalmist is right: "The Lord is good. His steadfast love endures forever and His faithfulness to all generations." Amen.